BLUE & WHITE

and other stories

FOR THIRTY-FIVE YEARS

WILLIAM YEOWARD

BLUE & WHITE
and other stories

a personal journey through colour

CICO BOOKS
LONDON NEW YORK

Published in 2017 by CICO Books
An imprint of Ryland Peters & Small Ltd

20–21 Jockey's Fields
London WC1R 4BW

341 E 116th St
New York, NY 10029

www.rylandpeters.com

10 9 8 7 6 5 4 3 2 1

A CIP catalogue record for this book is available from the Library of
Congress and the British Library.

ISBN: 978 1 78249 474 4

Printed in China

Words by: Alexandra Parsons
Designer: Louise Leffler
Photography: Gavin Kingcome and William Yeoward, except for
pages 5 (left), 18–22, 24–28, 30–33, and 90–95 by Chris Everard;
pages 184–187 by timeincukcontent.com
Endpaper illustration: Lisa Gibson-Keynes

In-house editor: Anna Galkina
Art director: Sally Powell
Head of production: Patricia Harrington
Publishing manager: Penny Craig
Publisher: Cindy Richards

CONTENTS

INTRODUCTION

What started out as a book about colour has morphed into something much more personal. This is a story of ten years of work, edited and distilled to produce a reference work of visual thought processes – the core, if you like, of what inspires me. It's an accurate reflection of where I am today. I know that design is an individual perspective, and I often quote my own words back to myself: design is an opinion, and this happens to be mine. But I hope that what I've managed to do here is to share with the reader the stimulating urgency of colour. With this book I also want to share a way of seeing colour afresh through a delight in our everyday surroundings – from a stone on a beach, to a book cover, to a scrap of coloured paper blowing in the wind – that may hopefully inspire a new perspective. The book is peppered with these visual incidents, recorded by me on a daily basis and ordered through the story.

When the idea of a book on colour was put to me, my first thought was to concentrate on blue and white. These colours are my cornerstone, my neutrals, my platform. They are colours that go beyond fashion because blue and white is part of all human experience – blue sky, blue ocean, white clouds, blue jeans, white shirts – it's a default setting. However, the blue and white combo has other credentials. It's crisp and graphic, spiritual, peaceful and calming and it will be around for far longer than we are.

The next great natural colour is green. Green, when you think of it, takes up a great deal of the planet, from snowdrops in the park to the vast forests of Malaysia, and it comes in all shades from dark pine greens to bright limes and the appetising crunch of young lettuces. It's a colour that has a trajectory, a beginning, a middle and an end – reflecting the cycle of life, from promising shoots through to full glorious bloom to the darker shades of winter.

Moving along from that gloomy thought to the most optimistic of colours, red, and all the earthy colours associated with it, from rich soil to glorious orange sunsets, violent violet and the palest blush of salmon pink. These are the magic colours of the spectrum, and for the designer to introduce these colours into the artistic world of an interior is something to be done with great care and attention. There are many pitfalls here for the unwary!

What lessons do we learn from observing colour so closely? The most successful rooms are those that evolve though the passions and interests of the owners, and develop and change along with the people who inhabit them. Think of really clever set design that so accurately reflects the kind of people the characters are that they do not have to say a word. So in the end there can be no right or wrong, but what remains is an imperative to express yourself through your surroundings. That's what gives a home its soul.

Through the brushes in my box and the colours in my palette, I hope I have been able to put down my thoughts here in as clear a way as possible. The message, if there is one, is to use these inspirations to create your own story. Enjoy the journey, as I continue to so enjoy mine.

William Yeoward

BLUE & WHITE

There's a whole world of blue: wild, primitive woad; reliable, safe, peacekeeping navy; that washed-out, barely-there of sky after rain; electric-buzzy, attention-grabbing neon; Yves Klein's trademark that's a work of art in its own right; grey blues that politely cause no offence and deep dark indigos you could almost drown in. For a creator and designer it's a gift of a colour and it is my pleasure sometimes to let it breathe – that would be where white comes in – but I am just as keen on mashing it about a bit and marrying it up with surprising partners.

White is not the simple absence of colour. Finding the right shade of white is a lifetime's study, and because light changes everything, texture is just as vital. For large expanses of wall and curtain, kind, warm, textured whites are easier to live with and more flattering to the complexion, but a judicious dash of harsh and glossy will add zing.

Blue and white together are a natural marriage, and while you can't make actual mistakes in putting any shade of either together, the result could so easily be predictable and dull, which to me is a crime. I strive for surprise and delight in everything I do, and that means playing with patterns, with scale and with texture, as well as my favourite shades of blue and white.

A creative eye is always snapping, and this collection of images is proof positive of my dedication to a palette in my favourite hues: a cohesion of blue, white and red summed up by the plimsolls and socks selfie. As it should be, inspiration is global in reach, ranging from India to Devon, Greece,

the South of France and a Gloucestershire farmyard. This montage, with its strong graphic element, is also a portfolio of my life's pleasures: family, music, art, humour and the British coastline – which I find more and more appealing.

JUST FOR TWO

This intimate blue haven is the interior of a tiny stone building in my garden in the country. It is a private, quiet space full of beautiful things and, inspired by the garden it looks out onto, is filled with leaves and flowers and floral motifs everywhere you turn. In design terms it tells a story about being bold with scale, about mixing vintage with modern, precious with simple. It is the antithesis of boring, matchy and predictable. The starting point was the vintage indigo linen tablecloth with a simple scrolling floral pattern. On the walls is a paper-backed linen printed with a vast scaled-up pattern – no point in being timid. And no point either in being intimidated by the Palm Beach peacock thrones, which add their own, surprising hit. I'm very keen on humour in decorating.

My blue haven is set up here for a very glamorous garden picnic *à deux*. Care and love have gone into every little detail, with candles glimmering in crystal on the sideboard and on the table, the table flowers taking a cue from the charming painting. The pink hydrangeas play a role in keeping the eye of the beholder from being too sure about what's going on here; it's all about punctuation marks.

OPPOSITE: **A comfortable chair is about as near to the ground as I get when out for a picnic. Memories of ants, grass stains, plastic beakers and dog fights are all forgotten in this fabulous setting.**
ABOVE: **Candle vases are practical as they protect flames from garden breezes. These have beautiful, sensual shapes, taken directly from the 18th century and heavily inspired by the foliage of the garden fern.**

I don't have much regard for keeping things in categories. An open mind, an eye for possibilities and a measure of courage are all that is needed to create something special. A slavish devotion to everything in a room being from the same period or at the same level of craftsmanship results in a look that is perfectly balanced, but where's the humour? This table setting is a mix of the rarefied and the peasant. Grand plates are set on a simple cloth and proper posh napkins are embellished with a rose from the garden.

The sconces on the side wall of my little cabinet of delights make an interesting installation. They are a motley collection of mid-20th-century French oak pieces found in a Nice flea market at a vastly hyped price because they were supposed to have belonged to someone special. Well, now they belong to us and something had to be done with them. They now display bottles by a French ceramicist, and buckets by an American artist, so they are earning their keep and doing their bit for global relationships! It is so important to gather from far and wide.

ABOVE LEFT: **Anyone can slam down a knife, a fork and a plate, but taking time to concoct a treat and a surprise for your guests is quite another matter.**
ABOVE RIGHT: **A charming detail in this setting is the seashell saltcellar, handmade with passion and care from seashells from the seashore! Passion and care are absolutely what this setting is about.**
OPPOSITE: **A tiny space that embraces surprises, wit, glamour, sparkle, candlelight and an informal straggle of garden plants – testament, I think, to the power of deep, deep indigo and a confident personality.**

PERIOD TWIST

Here we are in the Stroud Valley, a quintessentially English countryside of wooded parkland, dappled sunlight and mellow Cotswold stone. The house is a particularly fine example of an 18th-century wool merchant's home, set into the side of a gentle escarpment and approached by a big sweeping carriage drive that takes you up to the house, visible on the rise, and then swoops gently downhill as you depart. Georgian architects paid a great deal of attention to the placement of a house on its land, ensuring that owners enjoyed stunning views and arriving guests were suitably impressed. The exterior has been beautifully maintained, and all original details are there to enjoy, their job being to enhance the perfect, symmetrical Georgian proportions.

Inside, original panelling and ornate door casings continue to ground the house in its period. What the house needed was a helping hand to turn it into a comfortable 21st-century home for a collector of art and contemporary ceramics, while treating the traditional bones with the reverence they so richly deserved. Quite a challenge – and the key to the solution tuned out to be blue, the owner clearly favouring this palette above all others.

ABOVE LEFT: **The driveway, like a country lane, winds through typically English parkland, bordered by traditional park railings.**
ABOVE RIGHT: **The over-door pediments and the decorative window surrounds and lintels are typical of 18th-century architecture. The low box hedge draws a fine line across the front, again emphasising the symmetry and simplicity of this beautiful façade.**
OPPOSITE: **Here is where it starts to get funky! Against a backdrop of perfect panelling, painted a stone grey to take the walls back but let the details be, on an unpolished wood table, sits a collection of remarkable abstract blue and white modern studio ceramic vases holding aloft an irreverent arrangement of flowering branches.**

OPPOSITE: **Luxurious embroidered curtains enclose the garden door at the back of the house. The rug is a free-flowing underfoot interpretation of the curtain embroidery.**

ABOVE LEFT: **A real zing of modern art on the greige walls lets you know you've entered a house that's alive and full of beautiful things and colourful surprises.**

ABOVE RIGHT: **A welcoming sofa, covered in a printed linen and be-cushioned with an anarchic riot of different textures and prints, no two of which are the same.**

The eccentric pots and unconventional flowers are a first impression: further into the stone-flagged hall, there's a strong sense of something out of the ordinary going on. The furniture forms are certainly traditional and the craftsmanship is at an 18th-century level of exquisiteness, but the colour explosion is definitely from the here and now.

The owners' brief to me was "give us some colour" and I took them at their word. I chose this deep, deep indigo because it is a classic that will not date, a new neutral that speaks up against the greige of the walls and those warm old creamy stone floors. I didn't use indigo as a polite splash, I flooded the place with it, but stopped short of actual drowning. The classic lines of the furniture are reinforced by the level of workmanship that's so evidently gone into every detail, from the nickel castors and upholstery nails to the off-white painted legs that match the off-white of the fabric and the very smart white piping. It's as if their outlines have been drawn onto a background canvas. White piping is a decorative device that I use often.

The family sitting room in the
Victorian part of the house.
Traditional furniture upholstered
in a distinctly untraditional way,
the outsides are smartly pinstriped
like a Savile Row suit, but inside
there's a whole load of interesting
patterns and textures. In the centre
of the seating group there's a
conversation table, less formulaic
than the expected low coffee table.
Flower arrangements, as you can
see, are not "arranged" at all, and
are all the more charming for it.

The family sitting room is in a part of the house that was extended in the 19th century, so the feeling here is less formal and the proportions are solidly Victorian – strong, graphic and beautifully constructed. Blue is still the colour but here it is more obviously contemporary. The graphic swirls of the principal upholstery fabric were inspired by the shapes in sand as the sea ripples over it, and combined with stripes, spots and stylised florals, there's a lot of movement going on – but all in perfect harmony.

Possessions are on display: there's a playful distressed wood cabinet on the end wall, whose painterly interior is a perfect foil to a collection of ceramics, and the walls are hung with a successful mix of traditional botanical prints and modern lithographs.

The main focus of this room is the garden, The deep sills, piled with cushions, become the most desirable of window seats – a place to curl up alone and read or to sip tea and chat the afternoon away.

OPPOSITE: **The textured white rug on the old stone floor shrieks of luxury. The curtains are inspired by a vintage Japanese textile, with the elements rearranged and rescaled, and now completely at home in an English country house. The pretty round table has hand-carved legs delicately pecking at the carpet.**
ABOVE LEFT: **The real eye-catcher in this room is the mustard–coloured jug. I do love a surprise!**
ABOVE RIGHT: **The window seat cushion is upholstered in a luxurious cut velvet spot fabric outlined with a plain band of piping – no need to gild the lily.**

LEFT: **Your eye will no doubt have found its way to the astonishing bronze table. Every room should have in it a beloved piece of furniture from another time and place. Like the mustard jug in the window, it's an eye-catching surprise, and importantly gives a strong nod to contemporary artists.**
OPPOSITE: **The sturdy and solid cabinet on the end wall, seen in detail here, is made from bleached and washed acacia wood. It's a bureau beneath, a display cabinet above, and is reminiscent of Scandinavian furniture – lighter and altogether more modern and less formal than anything traditionally period. The wing chair can belong to any of the conversation groups in this room It has the same cut velvet spot fabric as the window seats, and a smartly tailored cushion.**

PREVIOUS PAGES: **Fresh flowers and daylight streaming in – a perfect setting for lunch. The dining chairs – which are supremely comfortable – are traditional in form with turned legs on the front, simple ones at the back. The upholstery design is inspired by rock striations, the walls by sand on the shore and the rug by clouds in the sky, so all in all, a symphony of natural forms.**
LEFT: **Table flowers with a difference. A group of individual handmade ceramic bottles surround the centrepiece. The Flowers are casual, the ceramics eye-catching.**
OPPOSITE: **Inspirations come from all over. Here's an upholstery fabric that evolved from a photograph of rock strata in New Mexico.**

It is totally irresponsible to have uncomfortable dining chairs

Nothing is new save the eye that sees it

ABOVE: **Apart from the real oranges, I've used orange mouth-blown crystal globe vases casually filled with daisies, and orange charger plates.**
OPPOSITE: **The table set for an intimate dinner sparkles with crystal, candlelight and a pop of colour. Important pictures need space around them. The little portrait on the back wall sits on a sea of blue, framed eventually by the windows either side.**

There's no point at all in having a dining room that only works by night. Lunch and summer suppers need a room that lifts spirits and makes the most of daylight; cosy winter meals and formal evenings can always be stage-managed if the elements are well in place. And so to the elements. This room in the Georgian part of the house is, as you would expect, beautifully proportioned with original mouldings and working shutter cases. The woodwork is painted with an off-white to emphasise the deep skirtings and soaring architraves. The walls are uniformly covered in a paper-backed linen fabric printed with a graphic depiction of ripples in sand. Not exactly a heritage wall treatment, but it is calming and harmonious and makes a perfect background for pictures, as well as nudging the interior towards the modern.

A dark rug on polished oak floorboards would be the expected way to go, but this is a predominantly white rug design inspired by clouds in the sky, with the traditional elements of spots and squiggles scaled up so it looks edgy and modern. In the windows, traditional side tables at a perfect height, emphasise the vertical lines. The very simple blinds allow the windows to speak for themselves, and for the shutters to shut. The round oak dining table has overscaled elements to it, notably the majestic pedestal inspired by a newel post I saw in a country house in the North of England. People always have some element they want to carry over into a new design: enter stage left the antique galvanised buckets – a perfectly irreverent touch.

For an intimate dinner, I have introduced an eating banquette, a two-seat sofa that is exactly at the right height for dining with a touch of velvet luxury on the arms and cushions. The table is set with crystal and a pop of orange, real oranges in this case.

LIVING WITH ART

Stucco-fronted Victorian houses are a particular challenge, with light coming in front and back and nothing at the sides. This client is a young businesswoman and collector of modern art, who knew her own mind and her mixed media. She loved the Yeoward look, loved blue and wanted her art to shine. Decorating projects often start with a mood board where we pin up swatches of textures, patterns and colours to give us a starting point. Bold and blue and natural forms got the client's seal of approval.

Small spaces have to be neat and organised, and this one also needed to feel convivial and be easy to live in. With all the blue and art going on, the walls were not about to compete. They were painted a delicate shade of greige – somewhere between grey and beige – a colour that's a perfect background canvas – neither startling nor boring. Light at the front of the house was a bit of an issue, so voile blinds, printed with stylised cartouches proved the right choice. The daylight could still struggle though, and against the light the patterns evoked a faded Venetian fresco, appropriate to a collection of coloured glass set in front.

Armchairs and sofas upholstered with a textural mix of linen, embroidery and velvet hold their own against the textures of ceramic, wood and glass of the art pieces. The surprise element here is the natural rattan shade atop an eccentric spotty glass statement piece. It's the humorous touch that's so important.

Smart white piping and buttoning give the sofas and chairs a tailored and organised look, and the mix of prints keeps the eye entertained. The art pieces left to shine here are the carved wooden sculpted horn shapes behind the sofa and the organic ceramics on the side table. The rug was inspired by a scrap of 19th-century German fabric. I recoloured it, changed the scale, messed with it a bit. It works perfectly here. Oak barrels with ebonised banding do double duty as art plinths and drinks tables.

37

OPPOSITE: **Going through to the back of the house allows a moment to appreciate the quiet presence of the walls and the herringbone oak floor, neither of which say anything, but yet say everything. Flanking the prints are a pair of reinterpreted Venetian candle sconces.**

RIGHT: **A frivolous yet substantial charcoal oak table is a surprise choice to display a pair of edgy ceramic rocks.**

Look carefully, and it becomes clear that design is about layers and form

Gone are the days of carting food from a kitchen to a distant dining room

At the back of the house, a pair of sash windows and a set of French doors look out over the small courtyard garden. The open-plan living kitchen is, of course, the epicentre of the house. In a rushed modern working life, some meals are grabbed at the kitchen counter, but there's no need to suffer on a hard bar stool while wolfing down breakfast or engaging the cook in distracting conversation. These bar stools are super luxe and upholstered in cut velvet, which plays off well against the marble countertop.

The small sofa beyond the kitchen is a good spot for relaxing with a coffee and a newspaper, or for keeping guests out of the kitchen with a drink in their hands while dinner cooks. One room living/eating/cooking is so much part of life now, certainly when it comes to city living, that carting food into a distant dining room feels like a world long gone. As this seating group is by a window, the sofa, table and chairs are deliberately light and transparent rather than bulky, the furniture is of greyed oak, the blue and white prints fresh and crisp, the framed painting neutral and charmingly characterful.

LEFT: **No surface is left unadorned. The bowls on the kitchen island are all studio art ceramics. If you need a bowl, why not use a beautiful one?**
OPPOSITE: **The bronze coffee table is practical and easy to reposition. It is also very stylish with a top that reflects the oak parquet of the floor. The rug is really strong and eye-catching. It's a design based on a vintage screen found in Paris that was covered in ribbons of different widths layering up, colour by colour, building to a deep indigo. The art that adds a touch of humour here is a gouache by Paul Maze.**

OPPOSITE: **The dining table is not in use except for entertaining, so in its downtime it becomes a display platform. The greyed oak table is a reinterpretation of one that I grew up with as a child, and it speaks to me of nursery food and happy memories. The printed linen blinds have the same build-up of ribbons of colour as the carpet by the sofa.**

RIGHT: **Monumentally beautiful, these ceramic watering cans are reinterpretations of 19th-century French zinc forms, thoughtfully glazed on the inside so they can be used for flowers. Grouped shapes always look best in odd numbers, so choose three or five rather than the dead hand of even symmetry. The tulips are my kind of flower arrangement, simple and just there, not tortured into a meaningful statement.**

My design mantra is to have one foot in the past, one foot in tomorrow and somewhere in there you will find today. Ignore the past at your peril!

The decks are cleared for action, the ceramic cans stowed away, and it is time to delight and enchant with a table setting that speaks of luxurious summer entertaining with a contemporary edge. The rug demands attention, but it does not overwhelm the whole. It is a design based on the worn and wonky paving stones of the streets of Venice. The dining chairs are really comfortable, encouraging guests to linger and chat way into the night. The backs are upholstered in embroidered linen, and the fronts, just to keep the eye interested, are an organic, free-form pattern woven into a textured ottoman fabric that is heavy and slightly ribbed.

In my design work, I am lucky enough to meet people with incredible skills in crafts such as weaving, dyeing, embroidery, glass-blowing, woodcarving, silversmithing and so on, and it's a joy to be able to direct these skills to fit the modern idiom. I find craftspeople all over the world – there are woodcarvers in Vietnam whose skills are on a par with the finest English craftsmen, and Eastern European glass-blowers making museum-quality works of art. There's a massive pool of talented people busy keeping up with orders for the traditional designs they've always produced, and I see it as my mission to drag them towards the 21st century. There's a bit of a snob thing in there, with people thinking that nothing can be more beautiful, say, than 18th-century silverware but just wait until you see what today's traditional silversmiths can do, given a bit of encouragement.

This whole setting, from the blinds at the window to the candlesticks on the table, has coherence and harmony, not because anything matches – very little does in fact – but because everything shares the same signature handwriting. There are surprises and delights everywhere the eye rests, but nothing shouts too loud. A well-thought-out blue and white scheme does give this versatility, it's classic and neutral one moment and giving off vibrantly gorgeous night-time sparkles the next.

OPPOSITE: **This tabletop celebrates generosity and hospitality, using the pineapple – that traditional 18th-century symbol of welcome and warmth – as its theme. All eyes are drawn to the centrepiece and the silver pineapple leaves. Table flowers are beautiful intense blue cornflowers with sprigs of spiky rosemary to keep the pineapple company.**

ABOVE LEFT: **All this glorious crystal is set upon a simple oak table with round rattan placemats. The lovely crystal seafood server presents the first course in a really simple way, the deep dyed linen napkins, loosely bunched at each setting, reprise the casual language of the ribbon blinds.**

ABOVE RIGHT: **Wine glasses are engraved with palm trees, referencing the pineapple leaves (every detail thought through – your guests should always be worth the effort). The water glasses are cased crystal, made using a process where a thin film of blue crystal on the outside is cut through to the clear crystal beneath.**

OPPOSITE: **The crystal centrepiece is the "wow" factor here. The cut crystal reflects and refracts light, and there's a lovely warm glow from the candlelit silver leaves that also sprout from the crystal candlesticks. These are serious pieces and they are sharing space not with fine white linen or gleaming mahogany, but with scrubbed oak and rattan placemats. I feel quite strongly that candles should always be white. I can't see a situation in which coloured candles would be better, apart from Christmas, maybe.**

I use my eye to re-examine traditional designs from all over the world, natural forms captured in photos and drawings, historical elements and simple everyday objects

MODERN COUNTRY

What makes a house great for entertaining? A first thought might be plenty of space for people to mill about, but that can lead to a soulless gathering with the odd knot of wildly animated people who seem to have known each other for ever and a silent majority looking in from the sidelines, wondering how to break in. The best thing you can do is force people into small intimate groups, where conversations flourish, people can be introduced and hang around long enough to get something started.

This country house has an enormous 10.7 x 6m (35 x 20ft) drawing room and, following my very own guidelines for a good party, it is smartly divided into seating groups, each with a slightly different character, but all in some way related. It is a room with a strong architectural character, gorgeous panelling and a late Regency marble chimneypiece that could not be ignored. Walls are painted in soft neutrals that tell the story of the architraves, cornices and panelling, but in a discreet, laid-back sort of way. The floor is covered with traditional coir matting, and the furniture has recognisable traditional forms. So far, so predictable. But for all the background elements, on entering this room you know you have stepped straight into today. The rugs are totally contemporary and there's not a hint of anything matching or chintzy. Fabrics are plain, striped or geometric, the bronze lamps and bronze mirror are modern classics with a twist. They are the punctuation marks in the story.

The palette here is grey/blue and the look is tailored and smart. All the elements relate to one another without looking as if they've been forced into submission. The windows are smartly dressed with printed linen blinds in a neutral colour with a lovely organic pattern backlit by the sun. These discreet blinds let the beautifully proportioned windows speak for themselves. It is a room totally at ease with itself and fit for purpose.

OPPOSITE: **Matching super-comfortable chairs but no matching upholstery or cushions. The wool rug is a white-on-blue striped check – the reverse pattern appears on fabric used for some of the cushion covers. It's an inadvertent reference that makes you smile.**

OVERLEAF: **One of the conversational seating groups presided over by a contemporary bronze mirror. The sofa is in plain linen with a line-up of interesting cushions. The armchairs may be the same shape but they are all dressed differently in mixtures of linen and velvet.**

Here at the far end of the room is the fireplace grouping where the atmosphere is more colourful and informal. The low comfy sofa is a very welcoming pile of squashy cushions, and the armchairs a delight of different textures.

All was going well with the greys and blues and little touches of mole and greige, when along comes a punctuation mark of red to surprise and delight the eye. There's a touch of humour here, too, in

the unexpected bookshelves with random piles of unreadable books. The owners are collectors of both traditional and contemporary art; one of their favourite artists is the self-taught painter John Caple, whose works are well represented here.

Atmospheric pools of low-level lighting are provided by floor lamps and table lamps. In a large room like this, lighting should be flexible, dimmable and flattering, especially after dinner!

BY THE SEA

Here is a different take on entertaining. This is the home of the daughter of the owners of the grand house seen on the previous pages. With a little assistance, she has taken many of the elements of her childhood home with her. This breezy seaside home has been put together with a lot of flair but not necessarily a big budget. It's altogether more casual in feel than the parental pile – it's got an air of The Hamptons about it – and a comfortable, tranquil, New England colour palette.

It is not a very big house, so every corner has to work. In the hall, a deep windowsill with a delightful view suggested itself as a restful spot to sit and pause with a glass of wine before the invasion of friends for lunch. My young client loved the blinds from her parents' sitting room, so the choice of a curtain fabric wasn't hard. It's the same design in a different colourway and printed onto a heavy linen that hangs just so. There is a lot of geometry in this house, and the square-paned windows are an ever-present feature, so I sharpened up the floral print with a blue striped fabric on the leading edge, to frame the windows, and featured stripes in the upholstery.

The hall opens onto a sitting room that runs right across the back of the house with three huge floor-length sash windows overlooking the garden. This room is young and fresh, and you can just imagine the furniture pushed out of the way, the carpets rolled up and the speakers cranked up to eleven. The easily pushed-aside tables are my take on the airy, painted Plantation-style furniture I saw and loved on a trip to the Bahamas. The simple voile curtains are hung on a rod, so they can be pulled and pushed this way or that to flutter in the warm summer breezes. I enjoyed finding exactly the right fabric – an homage to the square elements of the windows, but with an extra frisson of movement.

Good decorating doesn't come from the purse – it's a lot to do with make-believe and using what you have. After all, who wants to avoid fantasy?

OPPOSITE: **The bronze, screw-inspired table is the surprise element in the window seating setup, it's the perfect size and height.**
OVERLEAF: **The sitting room has a lovely seaside breezy feel. The rugs are the reverse of those in the parental home, light and bright on the lovely old oak floorboards. I don't think my young client will mind my saying that the urn-type lamp was a gift that could very easily have ended up in a cupboard, but it earned a reprieve and now adds a classical touch of the unexpected.**

OPPOSITE: **A touch of red in the curtain material enhances the warmth of the oak. The window frames a view of the most magnificent old cedar tree, a benevolent presence at every meal. A thoughtful surprise for every guest: an individual rattan striped beaker with hydrangea flowers.**
RIGHT: **The slate-topped kitchen island and a sparkle of martini glasses. It is not at all important to have matching glasses for cocktails – and these glasses could do double duty serving sorbets and ice creams. The bar stools have white linen on the outside to emphasise their shape.**

The living kitchen has simple off-white painted walls and the same broad oak floorboards as the rest of the house. It's a very relaxing setting with the French oak table and chairs all blending in seamlessly. The fabric chosen for the chairs is a blue spot linen, and in fact there's a triple dose of spots as the tablecloth is from the same linen and the pretty plates are cheerfully spotty too. The curtain fabric is again printed linen on a curtain rod, no fancy lining and expensive interlining necessary here. I gave the leading edges of the curtain a red border to emphasise the vertical, to raise the eye in appreciation of the tall glazed door.

The table setting is not in the least bit formal, but it is very pretty – all done in five minutes, and just in time to ensure the lunch guests feel welcome. The water glasses are etched glass, and simple carafes offer water and wine. The final touch was to scoot out into the garden and pick a few hydrangea heads to bring a touch of green indoors.

The kitchen island is topped with polished slate. It's a sleek and modern kitchen, but not aggressively so, blending in happily with the simple country oak. There's plenty of space for guests to gather round the island, and thanks to the elegant bar stools, it's a convivial place for experimenting with cocktail recipes.

THE PERFECT DRY MARTINI – ALWAYS IN A YEOWARD CRYSTAL GLASS!

N.B. Serious martini drinkers keep gin, dry vermouth and glasses in the freezer at all times.

Half-fill a cocktail shaker with ice. Pour vermouth into the bottle cap and pour into the shaker. Swirl it around to coat the walls of the shaker and the ice, and tip away the residue.

Pour in 70 to 85ml (2½ to 3fl oz) of gin. Swirl gently to get the cold reaction going, and a bit of ice melt dilution. Swirl again, but not so vigorously that you bruise the gin. Swirl some more, then strain and pour into chilled glasses. Skewer two pitted green olives onto a toothpick, pop into the glass and serve. You may wish to practise with the amount of vermouth – the more you add, the "wetter" it gets.

ENTERTAINING INSPIRATIONS FOR BLUE & WHITE

Ideas for hosting come in myriad forms, from the man-made to the natural. Blue and white are always happy together, but a dash of red is the deal-maker.

FROM ONE GENERATION TO THE NEXT

Roses round the door and an Aga in the kitchen – it's a perfect picture from a particularly English dream. This is a modest Norfolk farmhouse that has been in the same family for generations. The family travelled a great deal to all kinds of exotic places, but always kept this home as a base. They had neither the money nor the inclination to keep the house up to date with makeover after makeover, so it has retained its old world make-do-and-mend charm. The garden is a straggle of roses and climbers and lichen-covered walls, all of which is part of the magic. Then came the moment for it to be smartened up just a little with a few Yeoward touches to lighten and brighten but not disturb ancestral ghosts.

In the kitchen, the old range was taken out decades ago to make way for the Aga, but the shelf above remains with a characterful accumulation of old jars, saltcellars and soda siphons that defies minimalism and the modern passion for de-cluttering.

It is a kitchen that tells of lives lived. In the prize corner position is the rattan porter's chair where, shielded against draughts, Nanny used to sit when the children were young. In front of the Aga, an old rag rug covers up a long-ago kitchen disaster that's never been painted over, and on the way through to the dining table, there's a wonky wicker fishing stool with an interesting history, possibly concerning an eccentric uncle, whom no one can really remember.

LEFT: **The exterior is picture perfect. Fragrant honeysuckle and sweet-smelling roses intertwine across the porch and ramble right up to the windows.**
OPPOSITE: **The charming but basic kitchen with an eye-catching line-up of lovely old creamware jars and jugs at eye level in the Aga nook. Modern additions are the smart blue and white striped and checked cushions.**

Blues and whites, checks and stripes never cease to please my eye and never more so than when a dash of red is added

The timeless dining room leads off the kitchen. The walls are painted with a matt, textured limewash, an old-fashioned type of paint that suits old buildings well and allows walls to breathe. A simple striped dhurry adds a bit of warmth to the painted stone floor. The table is usually the central attraction of any farmhouse kitchen, and so it is with this solid, venerable piece that has accumulated many layers of paint over the years. Once upon a time it would have been groaning with farm produce, but now that the farmlands have long been sold off, there is water, there is wine and a fine glass dish of plums from the garden.

The side table is an old zinc medical instrument trolley from some long-forgotten hospital ward. How it got here, no one knows. The unframed canvas painting of a table set for tea is a charming thing – some amateur painter's forgotten work appreciated anew.

My contribution here was to upholster the chairs, not in anything approaching matching fabrics, of course, and to throw a length of fabric over the table. Nothing says "farmhouse" quite so loudly and clearly as a blue and white checked tablecloth.

There was a formal dining room in this house, but the old parlour off the kitchen was a far more practical place in which to eat, so the dining room was transformed into a sitting room.

The lavender walls are the same old hue they have always been, and the doors are painted with a proper old-fashioned gleaming gloss paint – nowadays it's strictly eggshell – but gloss paint you can scrub down with sugar soap and make it shine. Comfy, well-stuffed chairs and sofas have been upholstered in unmatched patterns, in the proper spirit of a house full of unmatched but meaningfully accumulated things. The curtains are a case in point: they are made from African Kente cloth, a patchwork of woven strips bought back from someone's travels. The seashore painting is another surprise, far too large for the room, but someone loved it, and its massive scale is engaging and involving, as is the rather glum young lady on the other side of the door, who will have people wondering what became of her for decades to come.

OPPOSITE, TOP LEFT: **A setting for happy times: an enormous welcoming table awaiting a gathering of friends and family for a feast. One can almost smell the aromas of a succulent roast wafting through from the kitchen. Farmhouse flowers in milk jugs – no pretentions here.**
OPPOSITE, TOP RIGHT: **Open-weave linen curtains with a slubby texture let the light shine through. Stripes range through shades of blue from midnight to azure.**
OPPOSITE, BOTTOM LEFT: **Old farmhouses can be draughty places. Rugs are thoughtfully provided.**

OPPOSITE, BOTTOM RIGHT **A collection of Chinese export pots on the side table, some with missing lids, but that's so often the way with family treasures. I love the Constance Spry-type vase on the painted Swedish table. It's an amusing piece, and the flower arrangement has almost risen to the occasion.**
OVERLEAF: **The original 18th-century dresser was too big to move, so it stayed, along with its lovely collection of 19th-century creamware serving plates and platters, quite lovely enough to earn a place on display in a sitting room.**

ALL ABOUT BOATING

Yeoward Brothers, founded by my great-grandfather and his brothers in Liverpool in 1894, was in the business of importing fruit and vegetables from Spain, Portugal and the Canaries. Business prospered and in 1900 the brothers launched their own fleet of ships, The Yeoward Line, soon expanding to include the conveyance of first-class passengers to sunny destinations atop cargo holds of exotic fruits. What could possibly go wrong? The First World War saw several of the ships taken out by enemy action, and the Second World War accounted for the tragic loss of several more. These were hard knocks to recover from, and the stylish, slightly eccentric Yeoward Line finally went out of business in 1954.

I am proud of my sea-faring heritage, and my brother keeps up family tradition by being absolutely fascinated by all things nautical. He owns a boatyard down in Cornwall where the family still retain a holiday cottage. Being the designer brother, it fell to me to refurbish when the place started to look threadbare and unloved. Of course I was my perfect client, loving everything I did. The cottage is tiny, the front door opening into the main sitting room, a parlour on the other side, and a small kitchen and scullery out the back. There's a sleeping alcove downstairs and two small bedrooms upstairs – and that's it.

ABOVE: **My brother's boatyard is nothing grand but it is testament to a deep-seated love of messing about in boats.**
RIGHT: **A trip back to the past. Yeoward Lines provided their passengers with all sorts of goodies to remind them what a good time they were having and to encourage them to tell their friends. Most of these items are sadly lost, but I found this playing card on Ebay.**

OPPOSITE: **This is an old potato box, once filled with delicious new potatoes from the Canaries. It has cascaded down the generations to me, and is now a box of inspirations, where I throw in things I like and listen to them talking to each other.**

A bit of make-do-and-mend on the agenda here. The mismatch of rugs is because these were the rugs that came to hand at the time. Mad nautical accessories include the St Ives poster on the sea blue wall and some little sailor dolls. I found a tin fox who seemed entirely happy on the rough-painted stone wall above the fireplace and a couple of amateur paintings that looked just right when artfully non-arranged. Fireside armchairs are a mixed bunch: one is really cottagey with red floral fabric and a frill, one is a slightly formal upright wing chair, and one is an armless modern chair. What unites them are blue, red and white stripes and the fact that they are all supremely comfortable. The open staircase to the left of the fireplace winds upstairs to the bedrooms.

The wall opposite the fireplace got a smart striped fabric covering and the sofa is now a patriotic nautical stripe. The side tables are a bit eccentric. The one you can see on this page is an out-of-context surprise that I found in a French flea market. It looks like an unfinished wooden plank top with tree-branch legs but is in fact made of concrete. The French got very excited by the possibilities of ferro-concrete round about the middle of the last century and started getting decorative with it. They call it *faux-bois*.

THIS PAGE: **The sitting room is delightfully cosy, and everywhere you look there's some interesting decorative ephemera for the eye to rest upon. One of my favourite pieces is the little Arts and Crafts turned-wood table lamp on the far right of the photograph.**
OVERLEAF: **This end of the room is home to more decorative ephemera and more delightful amateur art. The seashore is an oil painting in a chipped frame from a local junk shop, and the bouquet of lilacs on the back wall is a memory of an artistic cousin. The rustic side table is a reconstituted workbench, and sitting on top of it is an Irish railwayman's retirement clock dated 1898. So nothing terribly smart here, just little bits of life and meaning.**

Design, of course, is only an opinion, and this happens to be mine

There is a simple kitchen at the back of the cottage, where most meals are taken, and there's also a parlour – which is the place to sit and drink tea with maiden aunts, to play cards or board games when it is raining, or to retreat from family life and sink into the generously cushioned deep window seat and contemplate the sea and ships. The neutral palette of the parlour has been generously infused with pink and red to create a contrast with the sitting room. The floor covering could not be more basic – it is black lino – and I saw no reason to change it. The embroidered rug was brought back from India by a well-travelled relative. It looks modern but it isn't. It's very artisanal and unusually graphic – a lovely piece. I found the old pine table with painted legs in the scullery. Once I'd unstuck the drawer, I discovered a cache of old, tarnished cutlery. It probably hadn't been opened in decades. New curtains, new cushions for the lovely Arts and Crafts chairs and a smart paper on the walls have bought this room back to life, without altering its character.

ABOVE: **The basic kitchen retains the original cupboards. It's a room full of memories of cake baking, jam making and fishy suppers.**
OPPOSITE: **On the parlour table, the simple printed cotton cloth has a folkloric air to it, perfectly fitting for a tea party. A lot of work went into the chair cushions – buttoning, piping, shaping – but they still look casual. One of the ways in which I pull patterns together in a space is to border the leading edge of the curtains with a fabric that appears somewhere else in the room. In this case the seat cushion fabric reappears on the printed curtains, which link up with the fabric on the walls.**

LEFT: **A perfect study in the power of blue and white accented with red. This sprightly cushion is made from four pieces of mattress ticking with an embroidered ping of red at the confluence of the stripes. The oversized pompoms I found in India – they were white until they found their way into a dye pot.**
OPPOSITE: **The art of the window seat. One wet weekend, several years ago, a weekending guest got out a paintbox and transformed the window reveals with trompe l'oeil tiles – each one a little work of art. You can see similar work on the lampshades in the bedroom on the next page. There's a riot of prints and stripes here, getting together meaningfully in the snappy double ruffle heading on the curtains.**

Never forget the importance of red

Upstairs are two small bedrooms. One could argue for keeping things simple and plain in an attempt to make the rooms appear larger, but my immediate reaction is to spring a surprise by over-scaling. Here I've used big, bold patterns and lots of them. A couple of nautical references have found their way into this glorious pattern-fest. The home-made four-poster bed in the larger of the two rooms is hung with a fabric that references elaborate knots, and a cushion on the comfortably upholstered chair is embroidered with crossed oars and anchors. This room is a riot of fun, with an emphasis on patchwork and a generosity of comfort.

Downstairs, a little sleeping nook leads off the sitting room. With just enough room for a day bed, it's a good place to retreat to for an afternoon nap.

ABOVE LEFT: **A colourful niche. Punchy fabric throws draw the eye in to the space. Luckily, there is also a cupboard, as storage is an issue in this little home.**
ABOVE RIGHT: **Hand-embroidered cushions, one patriotic, one reminiscent of waves. Framed on the wall is a pair of woad blue and cream knitted socks. Art is in the eye of the beholder.**
OPPOSITE: **The crazy bed even has patchwork on the footboard. There are stripes on the wall and on the rag rug, and also on the scarf, lovingly made for the child's papier-mâché rocking horse that just gets a look in on the right-hand edge of the photograph.**

MY BEDROOMS

This is my bedroom in the country. The four-poster bed was, admittedly, a bit oversized for the room, and the legs and finials had to undergo surgery. It's a copy of a 19th-century Majorcean bed with a simple frame in greyed oak, and it's totally undressed apart from a spotted voile curtain at the back. Four-posters define a space, but I certainly don't like being tied up and stifled in fabric, and I didn't want the room to look retro or formal.

I've indulged myself here with a robust mix of pattern: geometric, floral, stylised and spotty. Matchy-matchy is a kiss of death to my eye. The blue is strong and the white is kind. On the walls, instead of breaking out a tin of emulsion, I used the linen fabric of the curtains (before they were printed, obviously), backed with paper and stuck to the walls. The result is a lovely slubby texture that makes a perfect backdrop for some charming paintings.

ABOVE: **Once you have created a bedroom that is a pleasant place to be, you begin to understand the importance of comfortable seating. I am lucky enough to have a working fireplace in my bedroom, so the armchair and sofa, with favourite things close to hand, offer me a choice of blissful lounging to read or listen to the radio.**
OPPOSITE: **Blue and white is my favourite colour combination, so it is not surprising that it features in my bedroom. The bed, in spite of its exotic Majorcean origins, is named Morris, after a Jack Russell whose favourite spot it is.**

The chair, chest and bed are all designs from my furniture collection, which is a distillation of my travels and inspirations from here and there. For instance, the acacia wood chest of drawers is my interpretation of a Swedish 19th-century commode, but the drop ring handles and escutcheons are based on a door-knocker I found on the island of Hydra in the Aegean sea.

My designs are almost always about stories, and I love being surrounded by the memories they recall. The rug is based on a naïf painting of sailboats that spoke to me from a stall in a Parisian flea market. I kept the imperfections of the original in the design, and emphasised the wonky geometry. It always makes me smile. The prints and paintings, which I collect from flea markets, junk shops and even from the odd reputable dealer, do the rounds from room to room and from place to place in my life. Their job is to be the grist to my creative mill.

ABOVE LEFT: **Something old to go with the borrowed and blue. I found a table lamp in a Paris flea market that reminded me of work of the legendary interior designer Madeleine Castaing, described in a recent article as "wildly beloved but relatively unknown". It's my homage. The borrowed cross is from the Greek island of Patmos, and the new chair has a very short skirt to show off its fine oak legs.**
ABOVE RIGHT: **My bedroom is in the really old part of the house. It has deep window sills and gorgeous gothic, lead-paned windows. I like to think the language of the windows has found a resonance with the multiple patterns heaped about the place.**
OPPOSITE: **Flowers, vases and paintings keeping up a good relationship. To get that soft, been-around-a-bit grey, the chest of drawers has been treated with a distressed white rub.**

From country blue to city blue. The idea here was to create a calming, luxurious, masculine space. My starting point was a modern dark oak and nickel four-poster bed with a fabric headboard and a fantastical Shantung silk lining to the canopy.

The architecture of the room is Georgian, so there is panelling beneath the dado rail. This was painted white, and the walls above were lined with a woven fabric rather than wallpaper, so the light plays with the texture. The curtains are simple drops of fabric with no fussy frills or pelmets to obscure the light. The fabric, however, is far from simple: it is printed and embroidered so it hangs heavy and textured – in a word, luxurious. The bedspread is patchwork, woven in strips and sewn together. The overstuffed armless chairs, smartly upholstered in self-pattered cut velvet, perform the function of a footboard. Luxurious touches extend to every little detail. I turned the deep sills into window seats (I can never resist a window seat) and piled them with printed and embroidered cushions. The night tables are made to my own design and have the rough texture of faux shagreen inset into the tops.

OPPOSITE, TOP LEFT: **Many, many metres of silk shantung were used to create the effect of being inside a jewel box. It takes a high degree of skill to gather up the silk, pull it through a ring and create the "choux" at the centre.**

OPPOSITE, TOP RIGHT: **A serendipitous find: a pair of smooth white-painted plaster table lamps are the big surprise in this otherwise textured and patterned retreat from city life.**

OPPOSITE, BOTTOM LEFT: **The embroidery on the curtains is a deep, deep midnight blue – the closest I could get to black. The design feels like tracery and it gives the room a zip of energy.**

OPPOSITE, BOTTOM RIGHT: **The shagreen-topped night table has a modern scalloped edge. A cabinetmaker's show-off moment: the inside of the drawer is inlaid with marquetry polka dots. That is attention to detail in spades.**

RED & ORANGE

Red is a passionate colour. It's alive and joyful, associated with fire and strength, Indian wedding saris and zealous warlords. In an interior, a little dash of real red is probably all it takes to energise a room, give it a bit of spice. Red speaks also of luxury and wealth. Back in time, when peasants wore clothes of coarse brown fustian, merchants and monarchs paraded their status in fine cloth expensively dyed with cochineal beetle juice. Luckily, colour is more democratic now, and we can all indulge with the life force that is red. For inspiration, we only have to look at the reds that nature has so bountifully produced: chillies, cherries, bougainvillea, roses, pimentos, tomatoes, pomegranates... just avoid any visual indigestion!

Orange is red's near neighbour – it's the colour of sunshine: hot, organic and warm, conjuring up images of bustling souks and market stalls piled with turmeric and saffron, bulbous pumpkins and sweet potatoes, oranges, nectarines and ripe peaches. It's the colour of fragrant curries, home-made marmalade and moist orange cake. A colour, like red, to use as wisely as spices.

A few subtle touches here. Reds and oranges are mostly a feast of clashing gorgeousness, nature at its sizzling best, and I love every manifestation. Here we have a good mix of the flashy man-made and nature's natural red harvest.

I'm particularly taken with the stalks of beetroot leaves, the translucence of a courgette flower and the succulent promise of a plump, ridged *riccio* tomato. It may be less exotic, but there's something particularly comforting in the orange-ness of a boiled carrot!

MOVING ON ISN'T ALWAYS AN OPTION...

A soaring reflective glasshouse was this owner's clever solution to the eternal extended family problem. The venerable Georgian manor house had extensive grounds, but not enough room inside for two families to coexist in harmony. This was a radical change designed to fulfil the lifestyle needs of today, and it has certainly done that, bringing in massive views from the floor-to-ceiling windows. My brief was to bring warmth and glamour to an uncompromisingly modern interior. No softening the impact with curtains or wallpapers or paintings – everything here depends on texture, pattern and lashings of light.

The seating is modular, so the proportions match and make sense, and the chocolates, greys and whites of the upholstery are calming but there's plenty of surprises in the fabrics, from the overgrown linen polka dots on the sofa cushions to the graphic patterned cotton on the armless chairs. The rug is one of my sea-and-sand-inspired designs. It holds the conversation group together in this massive high-ceilinged space. This was a room asking for a bold yet simple statement.

ABOVE: **A glimpse of the old stone manor house in the background. The low retaining wall of the garden skirts the new structure. The stones, mellowed with age, set up a fine dialogue with the glass and steel.**
OPPOSITE: **When the wall treatment is a garden view, the interior has to be in harmony with the great outdoors. The textures and colours of polished granite and old stone are beautifully balanced both inside and out. It is the punctuations of orange that bring the interior garden to life.**

The big surprise in this room is the fireplace wall, which is just stunning in scale. The fire was obviously going to be the focal point, so I took the colour of fire and played with it a little – less is more being a good pointer here. I've used just a handful of orange velvet for the cushions, and they're only orange on one side. They're just enough. I've used small bunches of orange flowers in small glass vases, I didn't want anything pretentious or showy because what's going to compete with that glorious woodland view?

ABOVE: **Bronze, wood and glass: more textures, more delights,**
and all in harmony with the whole.
OPPOSITE: **Here's the touch of wit that the room required,**
courtesy of a march of fire-red poppies in a variety of crystal
jugs and carafes. When it comes to flowers, I'm a strong believer
in letting flowers speak for themselves.

The success of this room is its unpredictability. On the one hand it's in the extension of a very traditional manor house, but it's not in the least bit traditional, and on the other hand it's in an inspired modern setting – all soaring glass, steel and stone – but the interior is warm and human and a delight to the senses. I perceive this to be a triumph all round.

OVERLEAF LEFT: **The fireplace wall in all its glory. This room is about texture, balance and flashes of fire.**
OVERLEAF RIGHT: **A study in black and white with a touch of spice: A curvy console table in ebonised oak with a marble top is a perfectly proportioned addition to this magnificent space. The tree of life table lamps are another reference to the great outdoors, and the black and white candleholder is an unexpected touch of eccentricity picked up on my travels.**

ALL ABOUT ARLES...

We could be lunching with Van Gogh here, but we're not. This sunflower lunch party with sun-drenched Provençal overtones, is set in an open-sided 18th-century barn deep in the English countryside. And the local climate being what it is, my guests were very appreciative of the vintage overhead heating system.

Taking my cue from the organic feel of the delightfully crumbling structure, I set up for my special party with an ever-expanding number of trestle tables. I used a mix of antique textiles from my collection, and a variety of rush-seated benches, stools and armchairs commandeered from the house, making sure that everyone had a cushion. The wild and wonderful tablecloth is made up from strips of African Kente cloth that have been sewn together, and the placemats are unhemmed natural linen.

ABOVE: **Mellow stone walls, ancient rafters and crumbling brickwork rather dictated the feel of this table setting, where everything melds together in a warm and welcoming way.**
OPPOSITE: **The secret to entertaining, well my secret anyway, is to be properly generous. I've opted for one massive, ripe Brie and an abundance of figs rather than itty bitty bits of cheese on a board. My Brie sits proudly on a classic glass tazza.**
OVERLEAF: **A riot of carefully controlled colour brings a ray of sunshine to an English barn. Sometimes a good party will benefit from a bit of organised chaos to stimulate amazing conversations.**

Cushions and throws make outdoor eating more comfortable and less draughty, and I've noticed over the years that a comfortable guest is a happy guest! The reds and oranges of the old bricks inspired this vibrant setting, and the ethnic textiles, with their lovely earthy colours, were the perfect choice.

Upon this earthy, ethnic base I've built up a shimmering tabletop dressed entirely with my Country Glass, which is, of course, no surprise! I like to mix up the layers of the table setting in the same way I mix up my guests. My formula is that everyone should know only half of the people at the table. That way you sit next to one old acquaintance and someone entirely new. Who knows where that may lead?

ABOVE: **Natural dyes, natural fibres and hand-weaving techniques... each piece is an appreciated work of art.**
OPPOSITE: **The decoration of a table should always be relevant to the atmosphere you are creating... although, I suspect, Van Gogh may have felt more at home with that yellow chair of his and his tin plate.**

It's important to get the contents of your china and glass cupboards to multitask. A vase isn't always for flowers, a stemmed glass not always for wine.
So let's get creative

It was a setting that called for the sparkle of glass and, of course, I happened to have just the thing: a range of handmade glass cut with a simple garland, as beautiful as crystal in every way. As it was a relaxed lunch and not a formal affair, I used carafes for water and for wine, rather than decanters. As placements, I used footed vases, which would be put aside to add to the general sparkle once the guests had retrieved their napkins and smiled at the sunflowers. For table flowers, I put roses, thistles and candles into a footed comport, a lovely small serving dish that could as easily be used to serve a green salad or a colourful dessert such as Eton Mess. The cheese, cakes and bread were served up magnificently on glass stands.

It's good to get creative with dishes, vases and glassware. Give yourself and your guests a surprise, with flowers in hurricane lamps, roses in teacups, napkins in vases and salads in fruit bowls. The next time you use the same glassware, ring the changes again.

TOP LEFT: **A place card could be tucked into this napkin and vase arrangement.**
TOP RIGHT: **The delicate leaf engraving on my Country Glass range just catches the light.**

BOTTOM LEFT: **Old-fashioned roses tie in with the vintage tablecloth. I've turned a footed comport into a hurricane lamp.**
BOTTOM RIGHT: **Rough linen, gorgeous glass and humble parsley – a surprisingly successful mix.**

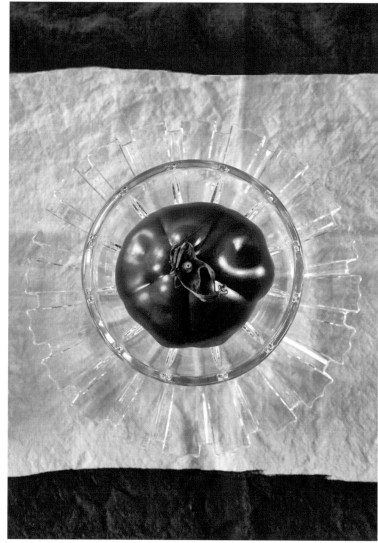

PARALLEL LINES

This is a story about a burst of colour landing on a marble tabletop in a strictly black and white London penthouse. The wonderful red and white battered linen placemats were the starting point. If I've said this before, I apologise, but I rarely have linen ironed because it zeros out the texture, which, I feel, is the whole point. The check napkins, left in a crumple at the side of the plates, add a bit of height as well as informality. The crystal is the king of the table, with straight cuts that add to the control and discipline of the setting. Try to imagine this room at night, with a block of soft overhead light catching the creamy white hydrangea heads and the broad, casual brush strokes of red – the warm candlelight shimmering on the tableware and dinner guests who, given the surroundings, were expecting something a touch more formal. That's what I'm about – surprises!

OPPOSITE: **A simply beautiful summer supper. The versatile crystal hurricane shades are set over plain pillar candles; they could equally be used over more elaborate candlesticks. But today they're being informal.**

ABOVE LEFT: **At each setting a crystal plate with a hand-cut castellated rim. The design is based on an antique original, but it looks cleanly modern, of course, because classic design never dates.**

ABOVE RIGHT: **The elephant in this room is the tomato. But how could I resist? Huge, glossy, beautiful folded forms created by nature. This gorgeous *riccio* tomato is nature doing what it does best.**

Embossed silver-gilded leather doors make an unequivocal statement about the quality of detail and finish in this stunning London penthouse. The doors open to a dining kitchen, shimmering with marble, silver and steel. Even the dining chairs, smartly upholstered in gleaming white leather, set up expectations of exquisiteness. It was in this demandingly severe setting that I prepared the table for a dinner party. It was a dream canvas on which to impose my vision, and my vision, as you will have understood by now, includes subversion, humour and colour.

The apartment is all about line and the neutral monochromes of dark wood, white marble, silver and black. There's no colour here at all, which means that any colour I introduced had to be able to stand up for itself and shout out loud. That's why I went for red. I felt that the marble tabletop was crying out for a touch of joy, a sparkle of crystal, of course, and a seasoning of wit. I deliberately got the contrast going here between modern severe minimalism and the general layering of life – but in a controlled way, respecting the symmetry and form of the surroundings.

PREVIOUS PAGES: **A room that has taken its decorative cue from a painting – an abstract expression of something that translates into straight lines and monotones. The table composition is made to look casually easy but, trust me, it most definitely was not. I took a great deal of trouble to create a tabletop that was in keeping with the calm surroundings, that was vibrant but not visually noisy. There's just one story here, and it's red. I really "get" red.**
LEFT: **Surprising doors that just say "all that lies beyond is exquisite".**
OPPOSITE: **Just a glimpse of the tabletop in the monochrome setting. Straight away you can sense a bit of a riot going on!**

WHEN COLOUR IS HOT

A classic inside/outside room in a walled London garden. It is a glass cube built to respect the late Regency villa it backs onto, so it's a link between old and new as well as house and garden. The room works well all year round, as the glass is up to the job of keeping out the cold, while bringing all the seasons of nature right to the fore.

I took my cue for this tabletop from the scattering of early autumn leaves on the lawn and from the mellow brickwork. I have a collection of colourful linen cloths, and these orange and dark brown sewn-together strips seemed just perfect. The rustic rush tablemats are in the sprit of ethnicity and, along with the grey napkins, fade into the background. The real story of this setting is the hot oranges, reds and purples of the art glass collection that populates the table.

ABOVE: **The cutlery was chosen so it didn't distract. This is a brushed-steel version of a traditional pattern. The salad course is a bold wedge of purple-red raddichio and a handful of basil.**
OPPOSITE: **A welcoming explosion of colourful art glass. The pieces are disparate but they are having a conversation among themselves. See how the handles intertwine and how the light-catching ridges repeat up and down the table.**
OVERLEAF: **Table and garden fused into one glorious natural experience. Art glass vessels twist and turn, adding both colour and form, flower heads punctuate, and basil, one of my favourites, scents the air.**

This garden lunch table is a celebration of both arts and crafts. The arresting art glass jugs are one-off and handmade, and mixed in with coloured glass they feel part of the setting, rather than a look-at-me add-on. There's craft in the plates, which are by a contemporary Italian potter who fuses coloured glass chips into the ceramic base, and there's craft in the wonky salad bowl, which has managed to be individual without being rustically chunky. The arty little knots of glass are a creative way to fill up spaces on the table.

TOP LEFT TO RIGHT: **Italian ceramic plates sparkle with inset glass – rustic, like the radicchio, but art all the same. Twisted glass baubles add zing. Jug and vase shapes look both contemporary and traditional, but there is always a twist. Fantastical mouth-blown crystal candlesticks from my art glass friend Colin which, like him, pop with personality.**
BOTTOM LEFT: **Glass carries light so beautifully. It's the basis of my love affair with crystal.**
BOTTOM RIGHT: **Nothing is complete without a touch of humour. I just happened to have a ceramic speckled trout standing by, as one does!**

This is visual colour overload, and I love it!

OCHRE & GREEN

These are the colours of the country. Ochre is the colour of iron oxide in the earth, and this natural pigment has been used as a form of decoration from time immemorial. Along with soot from the fire and dusky brown umber, it's the colour of cave paintings, early woven cloth and pottery. Ochre is the colour of summer and of autumn, of leaves and grassy crops turning to golden yellow, and fruits and vegetables ripening to edible perfection. For the modern decorator, yellow ochre speaks of warmth, comfort, sunshine and an organic connection to nature. It strikes up a natural friendship with whites, creams and browns and, of course, green – the colour of plentiful nature herself.

Green is a colour no one can escape. In the city or the country, in rocky mountains or verdant pastures, living shoots will pop up to embrace life. And what a wonderful variety of shades and forms that encompasses, from the plump little dark green pillows of succulents to the palest green of a spring bud. It says fresh, vibrant and ready to go!

Taking nature as a starting point and relishing, as one does, the colours of cabbages and daffodils, dusty green lentils and natural egg yolk, I should also add that man-made shades of ochre and green are yet another treat, with an intensity and zing that bring invaluable punctuation marks to any composition.

It's a saying that keeps repeating itself, but light does change everything, especially with nature's own colours of yellow and green. Here's a wonderful palette of sunlight on an English lawn, lichen growing in shade on old hand-hewn stone walls, a floral burst and a lovely jumble of summer squashes.

Let's enjoy the zing of man-made colours here: the masthead of my family's now defunct shipping line, the glowing gold edging on a fine porcelain plate, a poignant pair of children's shoes, a joyous graphic sign and a painted elephant parading in the streets of Jaipur.

ONE FOOT IN THE CITY

A new-build London pied-à-terre is the occasional home of an impresario used to sunnier climates. The apartment has been crafted with a great deal of attention to detail. Although truly urban, the English oak doors and floors were a joy to work with. Despite being brand-new, there was no compunction to call upon a particularly modern idiom here, as the beautifully detailed, classic surroundings were helpfully immune to period pressure. This was just as well, as my client arrived with some treasured belongings from his family and his travels, which immediately suggested a nod to the ethnic. His father's 1940s rush-seated sofa, for instance, once reupholstered, was easily accommodated, and the early 20th-century paintings felt quite at home.

I don't naturally do wallpaper, though I am feeling a modest calling, but here I wasted no time selecting a tonal abstract design for the hall. It picks up on the warmth of the oak and is pale and interesting enough to feed the space with an added dose of texture.

OPPOSITE: **A good injection of intensely coloured art glass pieces gives this impressive hallway the boost of *joie de vivre* that it required. The organic shapes of the bronze branch mirrors were a way of introducing an element of surprise.**
ABOVE: **A glimpse of the sitting room with sunlight streaming through to highlight the orange cushion. A compass is an invaluable tool to the designer and, at last, I'm learning how to operate mine!**

OPPOSITE: **I found it amusing to pair up the 1940s wooden sofa with a duo of Indonesian tabourets. The layering of patterns works well, reflecting the kind and gentle personality of the owner – no stiff, forbidding formality here. It's a room that is not over-stuffed, but it is full of energy. In the modern spirit of one-room living, the dining table sits behind the sofa, and against the hall wall is a limed-oak buffet that cleverly stores eight of everything, from knives and forks in baize-lined drawers to glasses and plates.**
ABOVE: **A mop-headed dahlia in a spherical crystal vase – a zing of colour perfection.**

Between the back of the sofa and the bookcase (I'm always suspicious of people who don't have books) there's room for a dining table. This one is bespoke, bold and chunky and patriotically handmade in Britain of silver birch with ebony stringing. The modern styling with traditional materials is a statement of harmony in this wood-filled room. The dining chairs are totally luxurious, and interestingly upholstered with a warm ochre cut velvet fabric on the inside and a smart grey on the outside. I believe that dining chairs should be as comfortable as beds, only upright. In my book it's a host's bounden duty to provide comfortable chairs, thus ensuring relaxed guests and good dinner conversation.

ABOVE: **The table is laid with crystal glasses. These exquisite flutes have cut stems and blown bowls, catching every glimmer of light.**
OPPOSITE: **With the mixed generations and provenances of furniture, paintings and objects and the eclectic layering of pattern, the room needed something to pull everything together. Step**

Shopping for furniture should not be a case of instant gratification followed by years of disappointment. Rather, make time for a careful decision, maybe waiting patiently for a bespoke piece to be specially made that will be fit for purpose and a joy for life

forward into the spotlight – the rug! It has a neutral background enlivened with dashes and slashes of colour, and it has texture too, like a line-up of pebbles on a sandy beach. It's made of two pile heights and textures, so the soft silky "stones" stand proud of the wool "beach". For me it was the perfect choice.

A LIFE WELL GATHERED...

The couple who own this small cottage – a basic two-up two-down in the heartlands of Kent – are a dedicated schoolmaster and his wife. They have led a peripatetic life as a result of postings overseas, and their home reflects their personalities, their basic thrift and intriguing travels. The decoration of the cottage hasn't been touched in decades – exposed brick walls and dark old paint have built up a patina of their own. So there are plenty of contradictions here. I was intrigued with the brief of helping them pull all the strands together and make a comfortable home for their retirement. We were working with limited funds, so I left the walls and the paintwork untouched, put up simple curtains on rods and concentrated on tying together their possessions with colour, pattern and texture.

I used ochre here as a neutral, as, after all, it is one of the earth's natural colours. It was the perfect bridge between the red brick walls and the dark matt paintwork. I chose shades between an almost orange and a greeny brown, which seemed to be in harmony with the ethnic bits and pieces that were so full of memories and the beautifully battered pieces of furniture they were understandably reluctant to part with. It is a simple house, and that's what I wanted to celebrate, while showcasing a life of comings and goings. It is one of my very favourite atmospheres.

OPPOSITE: **It should never be a concern if upholstery doesn't match. Take these two chairs: one is the charmingly battered leather original, the other was actually shredded and unfixable, so that's the one that got an upholstery makeover; the original had to make do with a new cushion. A necessary touch of humour comes courtesy of the carved figures from a wooden orchestra, music being a particular passion of my clients.**
RIGHT: **Who left the gate open? It was made out of chicken wire and whittled branches by a local farmer eons ago – a suitably rustic invitation to enter the little cottage beyond.**

OVERLEAF: **Another antique painted wooden sofa given the Yeoward treatment, and looking all the better for it. Please note the tiny, tiny spots of red on the cushion covers. The charming collage of children's self-portraits is a happy memory that just zings with energy. I have to mention the gilded bronze candleholders, because they shouldn't fit into this cottage at all. But they do. Who doesn't love a surprise?**

ENTERTAINING INSPIRATIONS FOR OCHRE & GREEN

A glorious spread of shades of ochre and green and colours that are attuned to them.
From the subtle to the crazy, there are lessons to be learned.

In the interests of thrift, the floorboards throughout have been painted, here using the same colour as the walls. Floor paint is a good solution if boards are looking a bit worse for wear, as re-sanding and fixing the originals can be an expensive mission, and anyway, removing patina is a social sin! Here, available money was spent on reupholstering a wonderful old Swedish day bed in an ochre-and-white striped cotton jute that's a perfect companion to the remnants of red ochre paint on the frame. This is part of the sitting room, but also a spot for overnight guests, who have been thoughtfully supplied with a bedside book table.

Next door is the study with an unpretentious wooden fire surround and bookshelves fitted into the alcoves. A woodburning stove is a perfect solution for people with busy lives, as it can be left lit and warming without endless poking and worrying about unattended flames. If you can lay your hands on a little olive wood, it will make for a really hot but slow burn. Two inviting chairs are a must-have either side of the fire, a case of necessary indulgence in upholstery patterns that pick up on the adventurous spirit of surrounding possessions.

LEFT: **The paintings are old friends picked up from here and there. I did manage to persuade the schoolmaster to invest in some contemporary lighting. The bronze tablelamp here and the angled reading lamp seen on previous pages add a bit of practical luxury. The fall of curtain fabric couldn't be simpler but the colour is a well-chosen warming ochre that pulls the room together.**
OVERLEAF: **The study bookshelves are stacked with well-loved and well-thumbed volumes. Over the fireplace is a watercolour by the owner, with joyful splashes of ochre and green. This room really holds together well.**

The object lesson of this charming little cottage is about bringing together a lifetime of treasures in a house that emphatically was not to be redecorated, meaning everything had to go with the interior as it was. It was down to my choice of colours, textures and patterns to fulfil that brief. I used predominantly ochre inside because, as we have seen, it's a warm, welcoming neutral colour. Some of the walls were painted blue, as were the window frames and the outside doors. So I took this idea and added touches of grey here and there – in the

ABOVE: **Some of the treasures that now shine forth: a fiery 18th-century Portuguese plate and a pleasing pair of 18th-century English ceramic miniatures.**

upholstery of one of the fireside chairs, for instance, which had the desired effect of pulling out the blue in the surrounding pieces of pottery and ceramics.

Playing with colours is a fascinating study. It's amazing how a tiny punctuation mark here can reference something in the corner of your mind, and the result just brings a smile to your face, while a jumble of colour that's not thought-through can leave you with a headache.

ABOVE: **Another treasure that can no longer be overlooked is this little 19th-century English spatterware vase filled with hedgerow flowers. On the chair, velvet piping adds an instant touch of luxury to the patterned cotton. The cushion cover was inspired by the idea of a pillowcase with a button on the outside.**

OPPOSITE AND ABOVE: **A simple, unpretentious picnic lunch is laid out on an unlined checked tablecloth. Napkins and cushion covers have been made from leftover scraps of material. It is a humbling example of make do and mend in the true British spirit that says just accept us as we are. The pomegranates are a little flourish of appetising colour learned from a lifetime lived overseas.**

JANE'S HOUSE

Sometimes a house and its owner fit so perfectly together that, by some mystical osmosis, the one becomes the other, and this is such a case. This house is Jane, and Jane is this house. The old stone Oxfordshire rectory is, like Jane, warm and welcoming and feels like a friend you have known all your life the moment you step through the door. It is set in the most beautiful, traditional English grounds with magnificent rolling lawns, formal topiary, a fragrant rose garden, an orchard and a beautifully tended kitchen garden bounded by Cotswold stone walls in perfect condition. The house is always filled with fresh-cut garden flowers, and the larder is laden with baskets of seasonal fruit and vegetables all year round. English country bliss.

Inside there are panelled rooms, open fires, wonderful threadbare Turkish carpets and fine traditional antiques that speak loudly of their quality. Jane wanted to gently refurbish without upsetting the family treasures or upstaging her disparate collection. I chose a colour palette of ochre and flashes of orange to reflect the flowers that Jane has used in her magnificent flower borders near to the house. In the library the plumped-up armchair and matching run-up are an immediate invitation to relax beside the open fire. The laid-back tones of the striped covers, piped with velvet, are a signature of Yeoward luxury.

OPPOSITE: **There is something wonderful about panelled rooms, even if the panelling is partial. It's all the decoration a wall needs – paintings would be out of place here. A useful tip from someone who knows all about draughty country houses: use coal and wood for the fire for extra heat.**
ABOVE: **The almost miniature overscaled proportions of this stone porch are in fact quite traditional in old rectories around these parts. It looks as if it were designed for a more substantial house, but the idea is to open arms and welcome parishioners, one and all.**

OVERLEAF: **The rectory library. The stripes used for the upholstery are all different, but there's a great language here, and a balance that isn't necessarily obvious. It's a balancing act that looks easy, but actually it is not! The corner cupboard by the fireplace is an anachronism really – it couldn't be more out of fashion if it tried. One of the things one has to learn in the decorating profession is that, for the client, some things are simply not negotiable. Enough said! Inherited pieces can be a conundrum, but I think you should either get on and use them, or sell them and buy something you really love to carry the memory forward, but that's something only the client can decide.**

Holding on to things that are imperfect is a particularly charming English country house eccentricity

In a corner of the sitting room there's a window seat, which I've piled with patterned cushions, the random colours carefully chosen to add interest and zest without detracting from the beautiful stone mullioned window. The window is obviously not double-glazed, so the cushions also serve to protect against the inevitable draughts. I have given the curtains a thick blue border on the leading edge. I often do this to frame the window and to link fabrics and furnishings together. This border, for instance, references the blue in the cushions, the piping on the linen upholstery and the intense blue glaze of the antique china. It is amazing the impact such little details can make in a room. Take, for instance, the pattern of the curtains. There is nothing traditional about it, yet it brings a sketchy impression of sunshine and flowers, and knowing that the room would always be filled with bowls and jugs and vases massed with Jane's wonderful garden flowers, it couldn't be more appropriate. It's a designer's job to think these things through and to remember that it isn't always summer outside!

OPPOSITE: **Beautiful antiques are everywhere. The round mahogany table is in fact a rent table, where a land agent would sit with his ledgers, quill pen and inkwell, secreting little envelopes of tenants' money into the drawers.**

OPPOSITE: **A comfy chair for an exhausted cook, thoughtfully draped with a blanket. In my experience of country houses, one's never quite sure where the next draught is coming from.**
RIGHT: **Resting on the Staffordshire plates is part of a collection of beautiful horn and steel cutlery – totally useless to eat with, as it could blacken a lettuce at three paces, but an absolute joy to the eye.**

Collecting is a great British pastime that should be encouraged and celebrated, and used as a basis for decoration and conversation

A beautiful 18th-century oak Welsh dresser practically fills one wall of the dining room. It's a lovely piece and quite refined – and typically would have been a gift at marriage from the bridegroom's family to the bride. It was, of course, both madly useful and also decorative. In the days before the fitted kitchen, a dresser was a symbol of status. The decorations here are uncomplicated – smart but simple striped linens – as befit an English country rectory, and the plate rack above the dresser is a showcase for that very British pastime of collecting. I do find houses with no collection of any sort a little spare.

Displayed against the whitewashed walls is a beautiful collection of slipware plates in magical earthy colours: caramel, chocolate and cream, each one a perfect work of art. Also secreted somewhere in that dresser is a pile of 19th-century Staffordshire plates with flashes of gold, ochre and green, which are used as Sunday best. They came originally from a massive service in a large country house, which was split and split into sets of more manageable numbers as it passed down the generations.

Another charming country house eccentricity is holding onto things that are imperfect. The tureen on the dresser, for instance, lost its lid years ago, and segued from table service to fruit bowl in one imaginative move. In the sitting room shown on the previous pages, the two candlesticks on the book table had each lost a partner but found a new life together and look perfectly happy with the arrangement. It all looks right because Jane made it so!

DINING IN PARIS

It's unusual to be invited to dine in a home in Paris, but I was lucky enough to enjoy such a treat recently and, as a result of the invitation, to see my work being appreciated and used. This is an uber-chic little apartment with a very controlled interior. The dining table overlooks a tiny balcony planted up with disciplined greenery in smart urban containers to make a shallow private space so that windows can be opened and that feeling of alfresco enjoyed.

Everything about the room is smart and chic, from the dark oak polished table to the understated leather chairs. It is an environment of crisp cut lines imbued with quality and luxury. You don't need gold and platinum and flash to say these things. It is a matter of what is not said that makes for the triumphant result. To my mind, the setting required a tabletop of exquisite symmetry and sparkle, and it took but a moment for me to bring out the lime green crystal to make the whole table pop.

ABOVE: **Nearly outdoors with the greenery in Paris. Lime green crystal reinforces the illusion.**
OPPOSITE: **The tabletop drenched with sparkle. It was lunchtime but that's no reason not to enjoy the added shimmer of a cluster of gorgeous candleholders.**
OVERLEAF: **Symmetry, discipline, balance – it's all here. The greyed oak table is the perfect platform for a sumptuous feast.**

Never worry about what other people think when setting a table.
If it is fit for purpose and looking right to you, then, guess what, it's right!

I chose smart linen placemats with wide stripes and understated napkins because I did not want to detract from the magnificence of the crystal. I think every table needs an element of height, and the obvious place for height on a round table is the centre, hence the shaded candlesticks, at just the right height, as you can see right through them. As you will have gathered by now, I am very much a fan of getting the flowers on a dining table just right. In this instance, I yearned to keep it simple and unpretentious, so I just popped a handful of stems into old-fashioned glasses. My hosts are fairly serious wine drinkers, and for them I chose fine-stemmed goblets with no decoration so they could swirl and sniff and do all the things that wine buffs do without distraction. Luckily, my knowledge is much more limited so I can happily experiment drinking out of many different shapes, both plain and decorated.

One of the many wonderful things about crystal is the cutting. I've learned to appreciate the expertise that goes into every stage of this craft and how light responds to every little nuance. Here I've used lime green martini glasses with horizontal cuts, and candlesticks with vertical cuts, and that seems to set up a rhythm for the points of light to dance around the table. One could get obsessive about this, but light is a wonderful medium to play with.

OPPOSITE: **When considering sparkle, one should not forget the gleam and glow of polished silverware. Table flowers should be kept sweet and low. It may seem quite perverse to photograph the desserts before the meal has been eaten, but when I saw these amazing lime green pistachio mousses, I knew that such exquisite examples of the patissier's art needed to be shared with the world. And, of course, they went so well with the lime green crystal.**

PINK *&* GREY

From the colour of a blush through to vibrant fuchsia, pink holds a fistful of cards. It's the colour of an English rose, and yet it is steeped in the cultural history of the Indian subcontinent, the Arab states and beyond. It speaks of warmth and comfort and embraces all kinds of emotions. Looking at a pink rose, I can smell the tuberoses, camellias and stephanotis growing productively in the perfume fields of Grasse overlooking the Mediterranean Sea, and I can see in one flower a multitude of hues from the stamen to the edges of the petals. It's bubblegum and knicker elastic, but it's also sweet peas, aubergines, pink peppercorns, hibiscus flowers and Himalayan crystal salt – all beautiful to the eye and the appetite.

Pink paired with grey makes a comforting palette. Greys are a perfect platform for displaying subtlety. In grey there is the translucence of sky, sea, opals, oysters and dirty diamonds, as well as the grounding solidity of rocks, metal and stone. So there you have it: two magical pigments, both of which display elements of softness and strength, a wonderful opportunity for the designer to create something far greater than the sum of the parts.

A multitude of opportunities to play with the depths of pink and grey and their attendant textures: driftwood sticks and stone, shells and mushrooms, shy flower buds and brash shiny mercury glass. Where does white stop and grey start? Where does grey stop and silver start? ... now here's the thing!

Delving into nature's cornucopia of colours, there's a pink-tinged asparagus spear and the grey-green spikes of a yucca. And how contrastingly smart are the man-made additions of aubergine velvet, nickel upholstery nails and bespoke suede shoes.

PASSION NOT FASHION

Given that a designer can only go so far to influence a client, and the whole purpose of the exercise is that the client is happy with the result, this summer sitting room has turned out really well. It is a lilac and lavender composition that has little to do with prevailing fashion, as the inspiration came directly from my mother's favourite things. It's a perfectly lovely and private place to sit, and it is part of an old stone building with no fireplace, which is why it comes into its own in the summer months. The focal point is the pair of south-facing windows overlooking the garden, so everything is oriented towards the view.

This is a timeless, classic room that is comfortable and welcoming, and it is what it is, evolving over time as the best rooms do. The curtains went up when the old ones faded in the sun, then one chair after another came up for a makeover. I used a lot of stripes because I wanted a fresh, summery feel, and stripes do evoke deckchairs, awnings and village fetes. My stripes are, of course, particularly smart, and there's nothing ordinary or predictable about them. They do their job perfectly and with great confidence.

The latest layer is the smart grey rug, essential as the carpet below was on its last hurrah, and about as modern as my mother would allow. A couple of floral cushions were also very warmly welcomed.

OPPOSITE: **A comfortably upholstered window seat, and not a matching cushion in sight. On the two-tier bronze table are some of the treasures the room was designed to showcase: the remaining two 19th-century ceramic apothecary jars from a larger set, long since gone; a 19th-century French porcelain urn on a base that once had a partner; and a hand-blown amethyst opaline glass table lamp, made by the talented Colin, my art glass friend.**

The idea of this room dates from the time long past when the lady of the house would have her own sitting room, away from the family, where she could pursue her hobbies, write letters, entertain friends and gossip over tea or a glass of wine. This is such a retreat. The furniture is arranged in easy conversation groups, and the furnishings, though a jumble of the new and the not so new, have all been chosen to be easy on the eye and to echo each other's colours and forms. These are smartly casual summer fabrics in cotton and linen.

PREVIOUS PAGES: **In front of the gothic garden doors is a most beautiful mahogany side table, and bringing the garden into the room are a pair of ice buckets doing duty as cachepots. The candle wall sconce is a nice period touch, and the bold and crazy pair of table lamps was a gift that adds a necessary touch of whimsy.**

The walls are painted a soft lilac, a hard colour to get right over a large expanse because there is a danger of giving the impression of living inside a boiled sweet. However, teaming lilac with grey, that most calming of neutrals, acquires a more serious, grown-up and grounded demeanour. All in all, this is a room delightfully fit for purpose.

OPPOSITE: **Fresh garden flowers in a crystal footed vase. There's every shade of pink here.**
ABOVE: **The rug is a new addition. It sits happily among the more traditional stripes. Touches of pink and lilac make this room sing.**

ENTERTAINING INSPIRATIONS FOR PINK & GREY

This palette is a gift. What makes it so easy is the endlessly versatile combination
of crystal and table flowers. Can you sense my passion?

CONVERSATION PIECE

I always work with the architecture of a house, but when it comes to the interior it would be foolish to be enslaved by the original uses that rooms were put to. In town houses, for instance, we no longer live huddled around fireplaces in small rooms, with a scullery maid beetling up the backstairs with jugs of hot water. However lovely the plasterwork and cornicing, sometimes you've just got to let them go. Interiors have to work for today's lifestyles and take full advantage of modern technology.

Here is a case in point. It is a calm and orderly corner of a sitting room in a London apartment, carved from a spacious Victorian mansion. It's a place to work, to think and be slightly separate from the world at large. The proportions of the original room and the windows have been respected and embraced, but this space has been screened off from the hurly-burly with an original Crittall glass screen divider. Crittall have been making their trademark steel windows with narrow glazing bars since the early 19th century, but this design is distinctly 1920s. It gives a feeling of separation – blocking out quite a bit of sound – without visually isolating this part of the room or interfering too much with the architecture.

It is now a very contemporary space, with a nod to the past in the form of a cast-iron "elephant" radiator under the window, powder-coated in grey to match the walls.

OPPOSITE: **My clients are a working couple, so in a spirit of equality, I used this lovely oak partners desk, which I designed specifically for the purpose. They have five drawers each to fill with all the mess of life, keeping the leather top clear for action. Little touches of pink and amethyst keep this space grounded in the domestic.**

Good contemporary design is more successful when it works in harmony with an historic aesthetic

The metal glazing bars of the Crittall screen give the room its theme of strict, straight lines – lines that have been artfully subverted here and there, especially by my Venezia rug, inspired by the crazy cracked paving tiles on the streets of Venice. The metal element is also present in the bronze table lamp, the bronze substructure of the buffet, the nickel trim on the partners desk and the smart nickel upholstery nails.

This contemporary space is home to a disparate collection of art. The two white sculptures could not be more dissimilar. The one set to the side is a stunning piece of modern studio ceramic, and then on the desk, a disturbingly eye-catching fantasy goat in a ruffled collar. On the streamlined mantelpiece is a trio of ebony candlesticks with bone insets, the shape inspired by the drones on a set of bagpipes. The model car is of solid crystal. All these touches are just heaving with quality.

Grey and pink are the colours working together here, the grey predominant for its calm and restful platform, the pink as little touches to bring a bright and welcome feminine element to this shared space.

OPPOSITE, TOP LEFT: **White on grey. The delicate porcelain skin of this holey ceramic piece stands out against the pale grey wall, reinforcing other touches of white in the carpet and the blinds. With pieces such as this, less is more. It deserves to stand alone.**
OPPOSITE, TOP RIGHT: **A printed voile blind, finished with a smart striped tape, is decorative and practical, shading the eyes from sun and giving privacy.**

OPPOSITE, BOTTOM LEFT: **A sweet pea moment, casually plonked into an amethyst crystal vase that could almost be a jam jar but, naturally, it isn't!**
OPPOSITE, BOTTOM RIGHT: **It is well known that I think people should be arrested if they do not provide comfortable dining chairs, and I feel the same about desk chairs. One needs every possible inducement to keep working. For reading, you need the source of light behind you.**

ALL ABOUT AMETHYST

The setting is a delightful country house near Bath, and the owners are a couple who entertain stylishly and often. This is an ideal room for dinner and lunch parties, facing out, as it does, onto a beautifully landscaped garden that looks equally appetising in all seasons. The soft grey décor of the room is a neutral platform, so it doesn't set the agenda. The curtains framing the garden don't interfere or scream out to be noticed. The dining chairs don't all match, but they make for an easy mix. The smart upholstery material is cotton ticking – again neutral but with plenty of character. All attention is therefore focused on the table, which can be whatever the hosts want it to be, so people never feel they've been to the same party twice; mind you, the food and conversation are always so excellent, I wouldn't mind in the slightest!

The choice of amethyst as the main colour here is interesting. Amethyst is not a particularly seasonal colour, and it's not attached to any of the obvious celebrations, like red and green, for instance, which say "Christmas" and "winter" quite loudly. It's neither overtly feminine nor masculine, but it is strong enough and interesting enough to make a statement – a pretty unforgettable statement, and a foolproof choice.

This particular party table is a marvellously confident mix of formal and modern with touches of tradition, but overall it is very relaxed. It is a perfect example of a setting that demonstrates the much-quoted maxim of the sum being greater than the parts.

OPPOSITE: **An unironed vintage white linen tablecloth and neutral pale grey walls are a good backdrop for an arresting table setting that's a riot of pinks and purples. A place setting always needs a bit of a surprise, so I've given the guests a tazza laden with luscious grapes.**
RIGHT: **The Vesper candlesticks, designed to hold tea lights, are perfect dinner companions, as the flame stays put, and you can see through them.**

At a good party, people will huddle together in intimate, convivial groups, and it is important to encourage this. If you want to throw a bad party, then spread your guests out thin

The linen tablecloth is the perfect backdrop for this amethyst extravaganza. The 19th-century linen napkins, lovingly embroidered with elaborate initials for a young couple's wedding trousseau, are a French market find. I dyed them the palest lavender, which subtlety underlines the marriage of the tablecloth and the crystal, or at least that's what I like to think! There is probably a special place in hell reserved for people who interfere with vintage white linen, but I anticipate being in interesting company.

I've used amethyst carafes for water, and the striking water glasses are double old-fashioneds in cased crystal. Serious wine drinkers will, of course, appreciate the vinous hues sparkling through plain crystal stemmed glasses. Table flowers are hydrangeas, and what a world of colour they encompass, from the palest greens through every shade of pink and purple and often on the same bloom. Gorgeous. In some of the vases, I've put just one flower head, and that works as well as a bunch, and they all came from the garden.

LEFT: **The texture of linen comes across best when it has not been ironed – it's not just laziness that keeps me away from the ironing board. Cased crystal is a fusion of art and light. Beautiful to behold.**
OPPOSITE: **The blue and gold dinner service is a new addition to my china collection. It serves to surprise the eye here. The blue really pops out, and the gold rim adds another kind of sparkle and a touch of formality. The amethyst vases are handmade in two sizes, so I've used them both for dynamics.**

Food raised up from the tabletop on a footed tazza becomes a special offering, giving importance to even a modest bunch of grapes

INSPIRED BY THE NATURAL

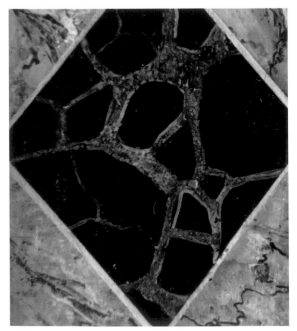

This is about the importance of black and white and the thousands of shades of grey in between, from a sea urchin to Robert the Dog and a papier-mâché mouse.

SEDUCED BY A VIEW

Here's a house restored with passion, without a thought to profit or commercial gain. In fact, "house" may be too grand a word for this early 19th-century laundry that a friend of ours discovered some years ago on the island of Corfu. Back then it was populated by goats rootling about on the earth floor, picking their way gingerly through the collapsed roof beams. It is in an amazing location, high up on the cliffs with a stunning view of the coastline of Albania in the distance. One look at the view, one deep inhalation of sea air perfumed with herbs and our friend bought this ruin in a heartbeat.

The plan was to restore the building rather than to rebuild it. The garden yielded up a lot of stones that had once been part of the walls, and with the help of local craftsmen, the old building gradually regained its modest good looks. It required a new roof, along with new windows and shutters, which were all sourced from local

suppliers and made with local materials, so it is perfectly in keeping with the original spirit of the little laundry. This exquisite dwelling nestles into the mountainside much as it always did, at one with the landscape, with only the modern amenity of a small swimming pool to distinguish it as a haven of leisure. In fact it is more than that – it is a spiritual, healing place where the connection to the past and to the land is evident everywhere you look.

OPPOSITE TOP: **The eating terrace, far from being spruced up with designer furniture, was created with a poured concrete bench and an unwanted table from the farmer next door.**
OPPOSITE BOTTOM: **The garden was created with a nod to the original layout and built with dry stone walls.**
ABOVE: **Lavender grey shutters are part of the local tradition round these parts. Harmony with nature is everything.**
LEFT: **The view that clinched the deal. The grey/blue hills of Albania shimmer in the distance.**

With the house now secure from the prevailing weather, the inside needed attention. The budget for interior works was almost non-existent, and this was much to the benefit of the spirit of the house, because there are no scary modern finishes, no state-of-the-art insulation materials and no fancy kitchen units. It is all very organic but with more than a nod to comfort. The grey walls are of washed plaster, and the floors of polished painted concrete. The ceiling is simple painted planks (which I have to say I much prefer to natural wood) and all in shades of grey – a lovely soft background colour. Imagine how jarring it would be if all these surfaces were painted brilliant white. The rooms seem perfectly sized, as they have volume, thanks to the ceiling height that has taken advantage of the roof space, and it really does make a difference keeping the rooms cool. Low-ceilinged rooms always feel smaller and more cramped than they actually are.

The house is really small. The kitchen with its double doors leads off the eating terrace and then through to the sitting room. Below the sitting room is the only bedroom and a

small bathroom, and that's it. All temptations to extend were resisted; guests overnight at the hospitable neighbouring farm.

The house is very uncluttered. There are no curtains, for instance, superfluous anyway because of the shutters. There are no unnecessary pieces of decorative ephemera. Everything here has a purpose. In the kitchen, utensils in jars may well be decorative, but they are essential to life. The lighting is very utilitarian. Overhead lights in the kitchen are a simple row of industrial shades; in the sitting room there are table lamps and floor lamps for reading and not a single LED spotlight in sight. How very refreshing.

The palette here is subdued and natural: grey paint, concrete, wood, metal and the bleached linen covers of the comfortable sofa and armchairs. It is a harmony of cool shades and any zinging colour comes from food and flowers, and the people, of course! My friend is the architect of her own confident style, and how most agreeable that style is.

OPPOSITE: **I recall many happy meals in this kitchen, sitting at the simple wooden trestle table. The metal chairs were thrown out by the local hospital and made more than acceptably comfortable with cushion pads. There's a row of china jelly moulds on a shelf, imaginatively used as serving dishes.**
ABOVE LEFT: **The airy sitting room, where scented breezes waft through the open doors. The sofa and armchairs, none of which match, of course, are all much loved finds.**
ABOVE RIGHT: **Looking through to the kitchen from the sitting room. Walls are almost bare of decoration. The organic shapes of local pots and platters are all the eye needs.**

CHRISTMAS & HOLIDAYS

Hurrah for Christmas! It's one time of the year to really let rip in the dining room. It's time to ferret in the loft, burrow in the drawers and pull out all those trinkets and baubles. Break all the rules, disregard the barriers between traditional and modern, dust off everything that sparkles and shines and rediscover all the rare and wonderful things kept for "best". A Christmas table does not have to be a cliché, but it does have to be personal, and it should most definitely have a sense of humour.

FAIRYTALE CHRISTMAS

OPPOSITE: **This is amateur dramatics, with spots of light pumped onto the pieces that matter, and that includes both the important crystal and the fluffy chicks. Electric lights were banished, but by candlelight, if you look closely, all kinds of colours are vaguely identified in the shadows.**

Time for some magic. For a family gathering, I pulled out all the stops to present the full tinseltown crystal and candlelight experience. I took inspiration from those rich, dark, Dutch Old Masters like Vermeer whose velvety layers of darkness are punctuated with slots of colour and shafts of light. I do try not to take my Christmas decorating too seriously. I'm not one for the designer tree with themed baubles. If Christmas is a family tradition, then it should reflect past history. We do buy a little bit of something new every year, but old favourites never lose their status, and that includes the slightly tatty fairy with just the one wing. Her place at the top of our tree is sacrosanct.

Full-on fantasy never disappoints. Be brave and never ask for others' opinions. It's all about you!

OPPOSITE, TOP LEFT: **A winter wonderland created on the sideboard with a quizzical turkey, some polar bears, greenery and red ribbon – never underestimate the power of a flash of red. The snow-laden pine-tree candles remained unlit – they were just too good to burn.**

OPPOSITE, TOP RIGHT: **The personal touch is important. I had a seamstress embroider the napkins with a phrase in my own handwriting. There was a different phrase for each guest, and that was my table gift. The little Crystal angels blessed every place setting. The water glasses are cased crystal double old-fashioneds, cut so they sparkle within and without.**

OPPOSITE, BOTTOM LEFT: **Traditionally in our family we eat seafood as our Christmas first course, which requires a spare napkin that gets whisked away after the fishy mess. The spotty spare is tucked into a simple woven cup holder – a little touch of the rustic.**

OPPOSITE, BOTTOM RIGHT: **Table flowers were hydrangea heads tucked into crystal hurricane lamps, and tall vases filled with greenery. And here's a surprise, a little bird perched in the foliage, just to lift the spirits.**

ABOVE: **I reckon I did pull off the Old Master painting theme quite successfully here. Gorgeous crystal comports laden with painterly grapes helped to set the scene, as did the red cased crystal glasses. Added sparkle and height came from glittering cones, and the cheerful little white birds complete the still-life masterpiece.**

MODERN ALPINE

A complete change of scene here, far away from family traditions of tinsel and crackers and dusty heirloom decorations. The setting for this youthful Christmas is an apartment in the Alps. Far from the wintering gloom, crackling fires, Christmas Specials on the television and the glow of candlelight, this setting makes the most of the sunlight that comes bouncing off the snow and streaming though the windows.

The goose is in the oven, the table is laid and the assembled company are spending the morning on the slopes to sharpen the appetite. They will come back to a joyously cheerful celebration that is all about energy and fun. All the traditional colours are here: red, white and green, but deployed in a very different way. There's a get-up-and-go feeling to this table, although, true to form, my dining chairs are comfortable enough for the party to linger until the New Year.

ABOVE LEFT: **Spiky rosemary pushed into footed hurricane lamps – it's a nod to the pine trees on the mountainside.**
ABOVE RIGHT: **A little festival-of-light grouping of green art glass candlesticks, which come in three sizes and I've used all three. The lovely graphic wooden Christmas trees that we buy for our shop are from the Pericles charity, based in Sussex, which helps people with mental health issues to engage with arts and crafts. Just a little reminder that it's good to give.**
OPPOSITE: **A joyful place setting, with a table gift nestled in the napkin. It opens up (just like a cracker but not as predictable) to reveal a groan-inducing joke and an amusing but useless plastic trinket.**

Most Christmas tables are laid with a tablecloth, but not this one. Going for a more modern look, I let the oval oak table take centre stage. Oval tables, incidentally, are really flexible when dealing with uncertain numbers of guests, as it is easy to add people at the corners without feeling cramped. This table set for six could accommodate ten, but only with a tablecloth: placemats fix the size of the place setting, and overlapping mats are never a good look. So let's see whom they drag home from the ski-lift! Another good thing about this table is the eye-catching steel base, which adds to the contemporary look and, at a practical level, means that no one has to wrap themselves uncomfortably around a table leg.

There are no traditional flowers on this table. Instead, I've used olive branches and generous bunches of rosemary and grapes – all lovely celebratory shades of green, from the translucence of the grapes through to the blue/grey of the olive leaves. The reindeer table gifts were just an inspired find.

OPPOSITE: **Winter sunlight sparkles on a table set with clear crystal. Festive red candles are about the only nod to the traditional family Christmas going on back home, and, only because it is Christmas, I relaxed my "white candles only" rule.**

TOP: **This is a particularly good napkin and placemat combination. They are fresh, kind of Christmassy, graphic and amusing. What more could one ask? The little skiers are tree ornaments but, with their hanging strings cut off, they seemed perfectly at ease slaloming expertly along the table.**

BOTTOM: **Black olives to nibble, offered up in a crystal tazza with a leafy sprig.**

A TOAST TO TRADITION

Christmas is, of course, the one time of year when the decoration of the room does not have to speak in any way to the decoration of the table. The table is the star performer, and everything else just falls away. I've chosen red raffia placemats, just the right size to peek out from under the bone china plates with their thick gold trim – definitely a touch of the luxurious. The informality of the placemats is picked up with the raffia napkin rings – too much luxe can be counterproductive. The crystal is clear, and the tall red coupe cocktail glasses add their zing of colour and are perfect for all the toasting that will no doubt take place as the meal progresses. As this is likely to be a long and leisurely evening, I've used shaded candle holders that take tea lights, so there's no danger of the candles burning down to the wick before the Christmas pudding appears.

I do not set out too much cutlery. My view is that half a yard of cutlery either side of a place setting is intimidating and clutters up a table unnecessarily as well as putting people into a sweat about which knife and fork to use. For formal meals, I will put out the necessary implements for the upcoming course, clear them away with the plates and produce suitable replacements. Less formally, just cling on to your knife and fork like the French do – nothing wrong with that.

Sometimes it is right to relax into the embrace of Christmas past and go with the flow of tradition. A white tablecloth, cut glass and red flowers will never hit the wrong note, and it just takes a little twist to bring the party right up to date

LEFT: **At each place setting, a napkin, a rose, a couple of thistle heads and a tazza of luscious dark red grapes. I don't do crackers.**
OPPOSITE, TOP LEFT: **It's hard to tire of beautiful crystal. Lit from below the glass sends shards of light pinging round the table.**
OPPOSITE, TOP RIGHT: **Red, gold and white: the colours of Christmas, subverted here by a thistle.**
OPPOSITE, BOTTOM LEFT AND RIGHT: **The table flowers are amaryllis for their hedonistic sex appeal, hydrangea heads the colour of bitter chocolate, thistles for their sculptural spikiness and the dark inscrutable purple of their seed heads, and eucalyptus leaves for their scent.**

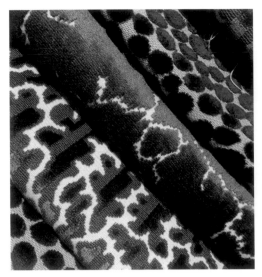

BLUE & WHITE

STEADFAST & TRUE

INDEX

ACKNOWLEDGMENTS

The list of people to thank for this book would be a book in itself since, as always,
I have had such support and encouragement. However, special thanks should go
to Kurt Levi Jones, Gavin Kingcome, Chris Everard, Katrin Cargill, Deborah Barker,
Adam Smith, Michael Nicholson, Sally Powell, Anna Galkina, Lindsay Cuthill,
Charlie Harman, Isabel Ettedgui, Colin Orchard, Cath and Hugh Padgham, Jacqui
and Douglas Erskine Crum, Tom and Danielle Ahearne and Gail Arnold.
Thank you to Alexandra Parsons who, through her words, has managed to
make me reasonably coherent and has been an utter joy to work with.
Lastly, thank you to Cindy Richards for another wonderful journey.